THE
I HATE
EUROPE
OFFICIAL HANDBOOK

By the same authors:

The I Hate the French Official Handbook
France: The Final Days
Saving Graces and Other Poetic Gems

THE
I HATE
EUROPE
OFFICIAL HANDBOOK

Denise Thatcher
& Malcolm Scott

*Soon to be Expanded to
Sixteen Volumes*

PRION

First published in Great Britain in 1994 by Arrow,
an imprint of Random House UK Ltd

This revised edition published 2005 by

Prion
an imprint of the
Carlton Publishing Group
20 Mortimer Street
London W1T 3JW

ISBN 1-85375-562-1

A catalogue record for this book is available from the
British Library.

Typeset by e-type, Liverpool

Printed in Great Britain
by Mackays

This book is dedicated to:
My Mother, Morgan and SAC

With thanks to:
Louise Cardwell, Brian McCabe,
Kathy O'Shaughnessy, Michael Batie, Mark Newlands,
Irena, Caspar Bowden, Janet and Morgan, Steve and
Mary, Karen and Sharon, Anjelka, Helene, Quasimodo,
Toshen, Georgie, Jonathan, Grimsmo, Alex at E.B.C.,
and Olga

And special thanks to:
Ian 'Mastermind' McLaren and
Peter 'Bendy Nose' Kenworthy

THE AUTHORS

Denise Thatcher and Malcolm Scott rank among the finest satirists in the English-speaking world. Both 49 and enjoying an almost symbiotic relationship, they dissect and probe to the very core of the overblown nonsense that is the European Union.

Malcolm is the master of detail, the forensic nailer of lies and semi-truths. Denise is the poet, ever-willing to embark, without hand luggage, on long-haul flights of fancy. For a decade and more they have collaborated on various projects including *The I Hate the French Official Handbook*.

WARNING

Many of you may find this work overly restrained and diplomatic in its treatment of Freddie Foreigner. For this, we, the authors, apologize unreservedly. Quite simply, too many underarm deliveries have somehow crept in at various typesetting and proof-reading stages (areas where complacent publishers have allowed large numbers of aliens to gain a foothold).

If you come to a section that seems somehow wishy-washy or namby-pamby, where you feel that the boot has not been applied with sufficient relish or back-lift, just read between the lines ...

A MESSAGE FROM A
TRUE PATRIOT

FOREWORD BY LIEUTENANT COLONEL
ANNE TREGASKIS MCC HIV (NEG.)

Europe ... God preserve us.

Many of us are not merely Euro-sceptics or Euro-doubters, we simply don't believe in the place at all. We are Euro-proof! When one closely examines what this E-place actually consists of, it is not so much a continent as incontinent. It is a disgraceful shambles of an apology for a continent, manned by bum-numbing bureaucrats, Mafiosi, Serbian warlords and, most sinister of all, Germans.

And, having created this most frightful mess, what do our garlic-eating brethren try to do next – disband the whole show? Not a bit of it. They want to cast wider the nets of their failure and ensnare the British in their cricket-free Common Market. Why? The answer is jealousy, pure and simple. Nothing is more galling for the Gaul or demoralizing for the sweaty burgermeisters of Cologne than to see Britannia amass a splendid solo innings on the world stage.

Freddie Foreigner is green with envy at our Royal Family, our naval strength, our wholesome foodstuffs, at the excellence of our telephone directories. Let him remain so. Should wisdom lead him to apply for membership of the British Empire, he will naturally receive a fair, if short hearing. But I say this, let him tamper with us at his peril. We may buy his sausage, but not his subterfuge. We may import his artichokes, but not his anarchy. Interference we will not tolerate.

BAOR Box 22
Channel Light Vessel Automatic
Herefordshire

The British view of Europe is based on ignorance and mistrust.
   Long may this continue to be the case.

50
FIRST-CLASS
REASONS TO HATE
EUROPE

——Part One——

1 Greeks sprinting (to their drug dealers)
2 Silvio Berlusconi
3 The Cheeky Girls
4 Norwegian whaling
5 Spanish donkey-throwing
6 Swedish furniture
7 Swiss arms dealing
8 The Munich Beer Festival
9 Portuguese men-of-war
10 Eurodisney

BIG TROUBLE

Europe, you may have noticed, is getting bigger. Ten new members were admitted to the European Union in May 2004. Why, you might well ask, did they want to join? So they could benefit from the 65,000 pages of European law that they must each now obey? So they could travel without restriction from Scotland to Sicily or maybe get involved in the European Space Agency? I don't think so.

The overriding reason why Cyprus, Poland, Latvia, Malta and the rest wanted in was to improve their living standards; to get rich – and who can blame them? The only trouble is that Germany, France and Italy, the big European economies apart from our own, are all in a serious spot of bother. The sums in Berlin, Paris and Rome have quite simply stopped adding up. And if the rich countries of Europe start to flounder, how does that leave the poor ones feeling?

Somewhat anti-European, I should imagine.

GREAT EUROPEAN CRACKPOTS

NUMBER 1
The Alexanders

German religious zealots whose fervour led to incest and wholesale slaughter. The entire family belonged to a sect which decreed that all non-members were evil and that only a select few of the cult themselves were free from Satan. The family comprised Harald, Dagmar, his wife and their four children: Marina, Frank and twins Sabine and Petra. At Frank's birth Harald declared that the boy was the Prophet of God and he was accordingly brought up as a young deity and worshipped by the rest of his family. When he reached his teens Frank announced that he could not pollute himself by having sex with women from outside the sect and so he would favour his mother and elder sister. With the active connivance of his father, the young Prophet favoured them rather a lot.

When the Hamburg police began to show an interest

in the charming devotions of the Alexanders, the family moved to Tenerife, where they continued to praise the Lord in their unique style. A few days before Christmas in 1970, Harald and Frank turned up at the house where Sabine was working as a cook and gave her some good news: they had just killed her mother and sisters. Sabine took this in her stride, but her astounded employer, a local doctor, phoned the authorities.

The police were revolted by what they discovered at the Alexanders' apartment. The small flat had been turned into a slaughter-house and, amidst shattered belongings and pools of blood, lay the bodies of the unfortunate Dagmar, Marina and Petra. Their breasts and genitals had been cut away and nailed to the walls, as was the mother's heart. Frank told the police he had struck the women down with a coat-hanger while Harald played the organ but that his father had helped him remove the 'offending parts'. The men explained that the family had often discussed the expected 'hour of killing' and the women knew that they would one day be sacrificed to the Prophet. Neither man showed remorse or guilt, quite the contrary. They were ruled unfit to stand trial and now spend their days in an asylum, their beliefs unshaken. Sabine was refused permission to join her father and brother and lives in a convent.

WHAT IS EUROPE ANYWAY?

Europe is like a visit to the dentist: it means different things to different people, but most of them are pretty ghastly. To some, it is 42 nations, home to 700 million people and stops when you get to the Ukraine. To others it is 37 republics, 7 monarchies, 4 crown dependencies, 3 principalities, 1 grand duchy, 1 papal state and 2 hard-boiled eggs.*

Take Turkey, for instance. Now, where's that meant to be? We read in a thousand learned history books that 'Turkey is planted at the crossroads of Europe and Asia ... a gateway looking both East and West.' That's not what I'd call a whole lot of help. The answer is to make up your own mind on the basis of the facts, which are these: Turkey is in the Eurovision Song

---

* Personally, I think of Europe as the place for which you receive five extra armies in the excellent board game Risk.

Contest and NATO. On the other hand, they all still wear baggy trousers.

Then there are those ludicrous places, the (former) Yugoslavia and the (former) Soviet Union, each of them trying to give birth to new nations that want to call Europe 'daddy'. Czechoslovakia, I notice, decided to become two countries the other day. What about Iceland and Greenland, The Canary Islands? The only bright spot in all this shilly-shallying, which for me has removed a lot of the fun from stamp-collecting, is that the number of Germanies has declined by 50%.

The big question, of course, is whether or not Great Britain is in Europe. To me the answer is both obvious and unalterable – you might as well ask if Halley's Comet is in my garage. Technically, I suppose, if you went back to a map of the Ice Age or something, you might feel that Europe was the nearest to us of the major land masses. But mere proximity to the scene of the crime does not establish any involvement. We are different.

We are not like them and we never have been. We are an island separated from Europe by cold water. We've been doing things here in our own unique way since records began and we've been managing pretty well for the most part, thank you very much. Sadly, there are some amongst us for whom being British is no longer enough. If you come across one of these miserable people, I advise you to do what I do when an Englishman tells me he is 'a European'. I tell him he's a scoundrel.

EURO-CULTURE

LEGENDARY POETS:
Rodriguez Placebo

The works of Rodriguez Placebo were suppressed in his native Spain for over forty years. To contemporary ears they may seem tame and full of Carry-On-esque innuendo but in 1938 you could have been shot for possessing a copy of *In and Out – Just Like the Sea*, from which the following poem is taken. A friend of Picasso and Pablo Casals, Placebo strove throughout his life to give his beloved people a voice, a language of their own, and, above all, to help them celebrate their Catalonian identity.

Her name was Catalina
And she came from Catalan
No man had ever seen her
Without her frying pan

Her squid were quite delicious
Her calamari too
Perhaps if you bring fishes
She'll even cook for you

F1, F OFF

Is it my imagination or didn't Formula 1 motor racing use to be mildly interesting? Dashing men with moustaches being killed on a regular basis ... sleek cars actually overtaking one another. What has happened? Why is Formula 1 now merely a procession of millionaires driving aerodynamic computers? I can give you the answer in two words: Michael Schumacher.

Herr Schumacher may resemble a human being but, take it from me, he is nothing more than the android alter ego of the dwarf Bernie Ecclestone. It stands to reason: if you were a vertically challenged billionaire with a passion for speed, you'd probably have created your own Michael Schumacher long ago.

The clincher for me is the fact that Bernie E, the Pharaoh of Formula 1, is the man who makes the rules, and while a car can be disqualified for having insufficient flange coolant separation, have you ever known a team to lose points for fielding a non-human driver or, as some call him, a German?

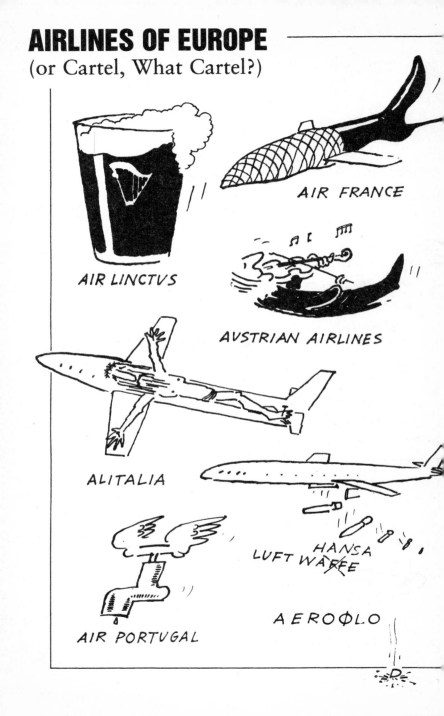

AIRLINES OF EUROPE
(or Cartel, What Cartel?)

BRITISH AIRWAYS

ROYAL DANISH AIRLINES

SPANISH FLY

SABENA

KLM

SWISSAIR

OLYMPIC AIRWAYS

THE
MANIFESTO
OF BENT

THE BRITISH EUROPE
NO THANKS MOVEMENT

1 Never (upon pain of instant deportation) to refer to the UK as being in or part of Europe.

2 To endeavour at all times to halt the disease of creeping Europeanization.

3 To picket at least once a month an international airport or European airline office (banners available).

4 To resist by all means the onslaught of the Rabies Link (or Channel) Tunnel.

5 To press Her Majesty's (so-called) Government for the immediate and permanent severing of diplomatic relations with Brussels.

6 To work tirelessly for the reunification of the British Empire.

7 To listen wherever practicable to the World Service of the BBC and especially to repeats of *Just a Minute*.

Be warned: several other organizations and groups are desperate for your support. Do not give them the time of day. I refer here in particular to BUTTOCK, Britain Under Threat To Overseas Cami-Knickers and UKIP, Unemployed Kilroy's Imbecile Partisans. Only BENT really understands how you feel. Only BENT can straighten out this Europe business once and for all.

FOR FURTHER INFORMATION WRITE TO:

Mr Eric Cleverly, Membership Secretary
The Scoreboard (Danone Yogurt End)
Edgbaston
Warwickshire

HEROES OF EUROPE

Frère Toblerone
1627–73

The legendary Swiss poet and lichen cataloguer to whom we are forever grateful for the following –

> *Oh rose thou art nice*
> *And pleasant to boot*
> *If I was musical*
> *I'd get out my flute*

– was executed on the slopes of Mont Blanc for failing to exorcise avalanches along the route of the papal progress of Clement VI. He was dispatched by the traditional method – being stoned to death with snowballs thrown only by the left-handed.

INSIDE EUROPE

What better way to find out what Freddie Foreigner really thinks than to take pot luck in the European press? Below is a totally random selection of letters to the editors of various Euro-organs, all printed on 21 October 2004. Here, for instance, we find a letter that appeared in Toledo's leading liberal daily *La Manana*:

> Señor,
>
> May I beg the permission to say you please about my funny experiment en Inglaterra. Well well, I was walking around Londres when I saw a jorse and cart standing outside a pub bringing beer into it. So of course I had to kick him in the cojones as I went past when suddenly come up to me a man, I don't know him, and he say, 'Excuse me, what you think you bloody doing?' Naturally, as he had put into question both my jorsemanship and my honour, I had no alternative but re-arrange his cojones for his troubles.

On account of this tiny business I am incredibly deported and the Spanish Tourist Office in Londres must find a new jefe de public relaciones.

Reciba un atento saludo,
Juan-Tapas Velazquez

For an insight into current Greek philosophy, the following in the Piraeus weekly *Tos Letticos* may be instructive:

Mi editos,

You may be amazed to learn but recently I 'enjoyed' a visit from an EC Health Inspector at my small hotel café-disco water-skiing farm on Sphinctos. I gave the fellow an ouzo, and showed him round a bit when he start to ask all sorts of questions – Why is the olive press in the lavatory? Do I always make taramasalata in the bidet? Do I wash my feet before I press the yogurt?

Did we not invent democracy? Who are these interfering Persians?

Yours,
Aristophanes Periscopolous

The last time Britain went into Europe with any degree of success was on 6 June 1944.
DAILY EXPRESS

Germany too has a flourishing press. This from the pages of the Spandau *Sportz Gazetten*:

Mein Herr,

Volkswagen, Audi, Mercedes-Benz, Porsche, BMW, all these motor vehicles I have many years been driving and not one time I am breaking down (excepting the occasion when an empty gasoline tank is provided by my ex-wife).

Now my satellite brings me the English funnyman Jeremy Clarkson. 'Oh ho ho, let us all laugh now because the German people are very dull and lost the war.' Perhaps, Mr Clarkson, when you are in your kaput Rover, waiting on the hard shoulder for breakdown assistance, you will not quite so loudly be laughing.

Ludwig Stickler

What price this Euro-sob story from *Il Testostero*, published in Naples?

Sir,

Silvio Berlusconi, our esteemed Presidente, has six television stations, seven swimming pools and eight new hairs sprouting from his head. When he has finished eating gnocchi with Antonio Blair, how many years do you think he should go to prison?

Massimo Stiffado, Pompeii

The weekly *Pas de Calais* has the distinction of being the Euro-organ published closest to our shores. This is from a far-from-disgruntled Eurotunnel worker:

Institute de renal-therapie
Hopital Generale
Calais sur mer

Messieur,

I'd just like to tell your readers what a wonderful time I had helping to build Le Tunnel. Everything was magnificently arrange. At eleven, small canapés of pâté de campagne *would miraculously arrive with our café. As you can imagine, one or two of the boys had brought their hip-flasks, well charged with Calvados, and so by the time luncheon was served we were in good appetite.*

I never ate less than four courses and for an entire month I never tasted the same dish twice. Such seafood and crustaceans I have only eaten in my dreams, and very special dreams at that. Et les vins! *The bouquet of a certain* '81 Pouilly Nouilly Brouilly *will stay with me for all my life.*

Then it was back to some good honest work as we wondered what they could possibly tempt us with for our pause-café *at 4.00. Sometimes it might be a delicately truffled raspberry meringue or a* soufflé Grand Marnier, *the other time just a simple* tarte au chocolat. *But whatever, we could be sure of a good nip of Calva to see us through the afternoon.*

Suddenly we had broken through! Our hard effort was not in vain.

Je vous prie de croire, messieur, à mes sentiments les plus distingués.

Thierry-Préfère Le Coq

And finally from Poland ...

Ulica Piludskiego 23
Szczebrzeszyn

My dear Sir,

I return to our blessed homeland from Anglia now one week. The Anglicy they are funny people. One morning I make an affair with the optician for to test my eyes. On the wall are the letters of diminishing stature which I start to read ... G, R, A, Z, Y, N, C, Z, K, A.
It is my sister!

Yours faithfully,
Przemyslaw Nowak

INTERESTING
BELGIANS

NUMBER 1
Aspel de Misster

If you're looking for a reliable supplier of office stationery or a competent chap to run a single-storey carpark, you can do no better than employ a Belgian – French or Flemish-speaking, it makes no difference. For some reason Europe's automaton class all seem to have settled in and around the city of Brussels. Put it this way, John Major is a cult figure in Antwerp, whilst throughout the suburbs of Zeebrugge the polo-neck sweater sweeps all before it in honour of Nick Faldo.

And yet there do exist within the Commonwealth of the Walloons individuals to whom the term 'interesting' might aptly be applied. No. 1 is the innovative restaurateur Aspel de Misster ...

The theme of the Café Cornucopia chain which he owns is simple: to promote the ethnic foods and drinks of Europe and force the American MacBurgerHuts back across the Atlantic Ocean. Mr de Misster spends most of his time cruising the autobahns and byways of the continent in his Hispano-Suiza, looking for unusual, but undeniably ethnic, ingredients and recipes.

Here is a recent Cafe Cornucopia menu, in its original English. You should understand that, being a Belgian snack bar, everything is served with chips and three varieties of mayonnaise.

Starters

Pâté de Pithiviers

The famous French dish of beaten sky lark and other small birds in season.

✹

Seal-brain Sausages

Made from morning-dew-fresh Danish seal-brains and served with our famous savoury rice pudding.

✹

Ambelopoulia

Our Greek suppliers spend months over vats of pickling vinegar to bring you preserved fig-eater birds in prime condition.

Please hold them by the feet and nibble the head off first.

✹

Piexe Espada Preta de Escabeehe

Basque delicacy of pickled Scabbard fish. Yours with a free 'Yankee Go Home' T-shirt for every correct prounciation.

Main Courses

Rudolf Roast

Celebrate the festival of Saint Niklaus with our famous hot Danish reindeer and cranberry sandwich.

✻

Tetine

Try our delicious tender, week-old French calf's udder braised in its mother's milk and served with a garlic baguette.

✻

Agneska Churba

In our interpretation of this noted Bulgarian dish we give you the lamb offal, rice, raisin and yogurt sausages.

✻

Mother-in-Law's Garotte

We prepare you a delicious plate of Portuguese horse mackerel, full of calcium bones for your teeth, cooked in the famous red *vinho verde*.

Special Desserts

Juustoleipa

Finnish toasted cheese served in cream with cloud berries.

✳

Leche Frito Tocinos de Cielo

From Spain, fried milk with heavenly piglets.

To Drink We Recommend

Belgian Lambic

The special taste of this twenty-year-old beer comes from its spontaneous fermentation in large open vessels above which pigeons are encouraged to perch.

✳

Coisreal Longueville

A light dry wine from the South of Ireland.

✳

Amsfelder Kosovsko

Forbidden fruits – a beefy red wine smuggled from the barricaded vineyards of Kosovo in Serbia.

A GUIDE TO FOREIGN PARTS

Italy

The capital of Italy is Rome. Other big cities in Italy that spring to mind are Milan, Naples, Florence, Venice, Pisa and Palermo, not forgetting Bologna, without which so much of our pasta would be unappetizing. Italian factories produce Fiat and Ferrari cars, upon which you should neither grate nor sprinkle parmesan cheese. Big Italian cities are especially noisy because of all the horn-blowing, but the further south you go, the quieter things get on account of the Omerta rule or Law of Silence. Chianti, Valpolicella, Alitalia: writing poetry has always been child's play in Italy

> **DID YOU KNOW?**
>
> *For generations Italian men have gone to measure their genitals on Venice's Bridge of Sighs.*

because so many words end in nice easy vowels. Here's one I composed earlier.

> *Oh to drink chianti*
> *On my elephanti*
> *I'd be so gallanti*
> *Girls would throw their pantie*

The trouble with Italians is that they've never quite been able to reconcile themselves to the fall of the Roman Empire. Deep down they feel the rest of us are barbarians in dire need of their civilizing touch. A world of mosaics, orgies, underfloor heating and Christian blood sports is what the typical Roman of today is striving towards. He dreams of the steamy public baths, of dining on peacock, porpoise and swan, attended by slaves eager to please.

Unfortunately their current emperor, the absurd Silvio 'Caligula' Berlusconi, is just one Cornetto short of joining the ranks of the criminally insane.

GREAT EUROPEAN CRACKPOTS

NUMBER 2
Ludwig II of Bavaria
1864–1886

The Germans, more specifically the Bavarians, have been providing care in the community for their lunatic fringe for well over a hundred years. But few come nuttier than their Wagner-sponsoring, champagne-swilling, castle-building monarch, Ludgwig II. He was apparently strikingly beautiful, at least in his youth. 'If I didn't have my hair curled every day,' he declared, 'I couldn't enjoy my food.' His beauty, however, was more likely to strike the peasants of the Black Forest, with whom he would chat for hours, than his generals or ministers, who, he managed to avoid for months on end. Unfortunately for the peasants, Ludwig was prone to dropping by in the middle of the night, usually on his gilded sleigh, and eating them out of house and hovel. Their reward: lavish bouquets of lilies and orchids.

Ludwig's first great passion was music. Within weeks of being crowned at the age of nineteen, he launched a search for Richard Wagner, whose operas *Lohengrin* and *Tannhäuser* had moved him mightily. Wagner was not an easy man to find, as he was permanently on the run from his creditors. After their first meeting he wrote of the King, 'He loves me with the fire and tenderness of a first love, he knows and understands everything about me – understands me like my own soul. He wants me to

be always at his side, to work, to relax and to produce my operas … Oh, may he but live! It is an unbelievable miracle.' For ten odd years Ludwig bankrolled his 'Dear One': he paid off his debts, bought him houses, showered him with gifts and generally pandered to the luxury-loving artist's whims. The strange thing was that Ludwig was almost completely unmusical.

When public opinion finally forced Wagner to quit Bavaria, Ludwig turned his hand, which was never far from his cheque book, to the building game. Grottos, gardens, fairytale castles perched on rocky pinnacles –

all were run up at incredible expense and with obsessive attention to detail. To check that a particular blue in a particular grotto was precisely the right shade, Ludwig dispatched his manservant to Capri, twice. When the money inevitably began to run short, Ludwig sent off emissaries to find him a new kingdom that he could rule, and presumably bankrupt, as an absolute monarch. Finance for the new place – Afghanistan was one possibility – would come from selling Bavaria to his uncle.

Ludwig was nothing if not restless. This from the memoirs of Graf Trauttmansdorf: 'The King likes to imagine that he is riding to some particular place. He calculates the distances according to the circumference of the riding school and then, night after night, rides round and round from eight o'clock in the evening until two or three o'clock in the morning, followed by a groom, changing horses when necessary. After several hours he dismounts and has a picnic supper brought to him on the spot, then remounts and rides on until he calculates that he has reached his goal. The groom who recently rode with him "from Munich to Innsbruck" received in reward a gold watch and chain.'

On real journeys, if he wasn't knocking up the peasantry, Ludwig would sometimes insist on eating in the open air in a blizzard or in temperatures well below freezing. He would assure his shivering companions that they were at the seaside in the glorious hot sun. Finally they came to take him away, armed with a long document detailing his derailment. A couple of days later he went for an early evening stroll with a minder and the pair were found mysteriously drowned in the shallow waters of Lake Starnberg. Please now to hum yourself the Death March from *Götterdämmerung*.

And yet he did have his admirers ... 'If we take away from the Munich of today anything that was created under Ludwig II we should be horror-stricken to see how meagre has been the output of important artistic creations since that time.' Adolf Hitler, *Mein Kampf*.

It is not recorded whether Ludwig himself ever attended the Munich Beer Festival, that seemingly vital stopover for Antipodeans en route from Bangkok to Earls Court. Somehow I don't think it would have been quite his scene.

Massed ranks of cheery, bloated Bavarians breaking wind in unison, otherwise known as an oompah band; columns of synchronized sausage swallowers; vast-breasted, flaxen-headed waitresses power-lifting trayfuls of frothy lager, no wonder he wanted to live on top of an inaccessible mountain.

WARNING   GERMAN JOKE   WARNING

Q: Why is German beer made from only four ingredients?
A: So it is easy to remember the recipe.

50
FIRST-CLASS
REASONS TO HATE
EUROPE

——*Part Two*——

Ein Volk
Ein Reich
Ein Wurst

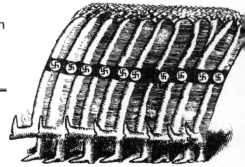

CALLING GERMANY

Who would relinquish Asia, Africa or Italy for Germany; a land rude in its surface, rigorous in its climate, cheerless to every beholder and cultivator except a native?

TACITUS, 98 AD

It is easy to make cheap jokes about the Germans – their militarism, their love of conformity and authority, their lack of wit. Easy but necessary. The great post-war boom may well be foundering on the iceberg of reunification, but there's still enough sauerkraut in the cellar to keep the rest of Europe on its guard. The Hun still means business. Turn your back on Schultz at your peril.

CONFORMITY

Family Fortunes is a popular if dreadful television entertainment in which guests try to guess what the audience will say when confronted by a word or concept. For example, given the word *bubble*, the audience might come up with the six alternatives *bath*, *champagne*, *car*, *cartoon*, *chocolate* and *squeak*. The format of the game was tested in (former) West Germany in 1986 under the catchy name *Verwandschaftsglück*, but it failed miserably. Time and again the audience was given their word and time and again 95% of them gave the same reply. The only word that the audience managed to achieve six alternatives for was *beer*.

AUTHORITY

Berlin in 1931 was not a happy place, unless of course you had a wardrobe full of brown shirts. To celebrate Adolf's arrival on the scene there were frequent purges, round-ups and riots, many of which occurred in Alexander Platz, a large square in downtown Berlin complete with fountains and lawns. Picture the scene: beer-gutted Bavarians slugging it out with cologne-splashed communists amid coshes, crowbars and broken heads. According to an eye-witness, 'The police arrived and slowly got themselves into formation – the fascists were winning that night – they waded into the mob with truncheons and rifle butts, causing it to disperse almost immediately. Hundreds of blood-soaked men sprinted from the square, communists or fascists you couldn't tell, but despite providing an obvious short cut, not one of them trod on the grass.'

It's not true that Germans don't have a sense of humour – they find Laurel and Hardy utterly side-splitting – it's just that they completely lack wit. Tell a German a joke involving a pun and he'll stare at you blankly. '*Das ist incorrekt*,' he'll say at length. Here is a German joke. Actually, it is The German Joke. Before you read on we recommend that you double your home contents insurance policy and arrange to take a week off work.

Q: Why did Eva Braun have to eat Hitler's sausage?
A: Because he was a vegetarian.

Remember, a German joke is no laughing matter.

German is the most extravagantly ugly language. It sounds like someone using a sick bag on a 747.

WILLY RUSHTON

EURO 2004 – THREE LIONS, ONE DONKEY AND A SWISSTLEBLOWER

Only one thing stood between the mighty England and glory at the 2004 European Cup and that was a bunch of bloody Europeans. Leaving aside the French and the Portuguese – as one should always try to do – our days were numbered from the moment Urs 'in favour of the Portuguese' Meier, a Swiss 'referee' decided to pull on his short trousers. Swiss neutrality, what a joke. The man is obviously a lifelong lover of grilled sardines and vintage port. And I for one would be less than astounded to learn that his Algarve love nest had recently received more than a lick of Portuguese paint.

Yet even this we could have taken in our stride had not incalculable psychological damage already been inflicted on our English giants. I refer, of course, to the

Swedish 'coach', Sven-Goran Eriksson. Now don't get me wrong, if I was looking for a tutor to help a close friend pass his accountancy exams, Sven would be high on my list. If tempers started to fray at a veteran ladies cross-country skiing event, I could imagine no one better than Sven to bring matters safely under control. But to lift the spirits of a band of red-bloodied Englishmen ... we might as well have had Hyacinth Bucket in charge.

The root cause of many of our troubles, of course, is the magnificent Premiership ... a magnet for continental players wishing to reach their full potential. Being a nation of sportsmen we are good enough to allow large numbers of speedy European toe-booters to be trained here in the arts of manly play. How do they repay us? With subsiding penalty spots and bone-crunching fouls on our teenage prodigy. Did the English bestow the gift of football on a grateful planet to be treated like this?

To say that Euro 2004 was an unmitigated disaster would, however, be wide of the mark. To watch the French flounder is always a joy and unless your idea of a decent game of soccer is to see a gang of hacking hairdressers passing the ball backwards for an hour and a half, then you would have been encouraged by the early exit of the Italians. The graceless Germans and the sleep-inducing Spanish both gave new meaning to the word 'woeful'. Hapless Holland, the pre-menstrual Portuguese ... Somehow through this succession of footballing farces the wily Greeks managed to oil their way. What a way to spend the summer.

The next big one, of course, is Germany 2006 – the World Cup. We've been there before, albeit in wartime, and we're going again. Tempers may have cooled in the past sixty years but Hans should understand we are in no mood to take prisoners. Nothing less than outright victory will be acceptable.

If things don't go our way this time, serious consideration must be given to enforcing a ban on the playing of football outside the United Kingdom. I know it sounds harsh but it's our bloody game and if the rest of you won't play properly then we'll just have to take away the ball.

GREAT EUROPEAN CRACKPOTS

NUMBER 3
Peter Kurten
1883–1931

Diminutive, mild-mannered Peter Kurten led a career of theft, arson and murder that reached a peak in 1929 when he assaulted twenty-three women and children in Dusseldorf. His favourite weapon was a pair of scissors and he sometimes drank the blood of his victims, earning him the nickname The Vampire of Dusseldorf. From an early age he aspired to this kind of notoriety – he first attempted murder before he was six – and during the many years he spent in prison he would fantasize about sado-sexual crimes. Despite this, his wife noticed nothing peculiar and was astounded when, once he realized arrest was imminent, he confessed to her and urged her to turn him in to the police for the reward money. 'It was not easy to convince her,' he complained.

Kurten was charged with nine murders and seven attempted murders but confessed to sixty-eight more offences. Before being beheaded in July 1931, he said to his executioner, 'After my head has been chopped off, will I still be able to hear at least for a moment the sound of my own blood gushing from the stump of my neck? That would be the pleasure to end all pleasures.'

America is Europe's delinquent son. What America needs to realize is that we are not too old to put you over our knee and give you the tanning you so richly deserve.

FRA GUISEPPE DI CAPRIO

SIX TOP EUROPEAN ATTRACTIONS

The Torremolinas Open

This prestigious tournament, sponsored for the fourth year by Cruddocks Yorkshire Pudding Batter Mix, draws golfers from several kilometres, many of whom have their own clubs.

The Benidorm Billion

One billion pesetas (e 3,009.69) goes to the winner of this floodlit handicap for two-year-olds sponsored for the fifth year running by Lavistop.

The Palermo Kidnapping Championships

Spend a week blindfolded in a dank cellar. Hack off your own finger or ear and send it to your loved ones. This highlight of the Sicilian Festival of Organized Crime is growing ever more popular with Germans.

The Oslo Rice Museum

Fascinating insights into this often neglected cereal of the East. Long grains, short grains, whole grains ... wade through a real paddy field with Bas Matti the elephant boy for a glutenriching experience.

Vladland

Stake out your place on a once-in-a-lifetime journey to the gruesome kingdom of Vlad the Impaler. Learn the secrets of Transylvania's zaniest potentate. Was Vlad really a mummy's boy ... Why was his nickname Veronica ... Did he invent the toothpick? Everywhere else just impales by comparison.

The Berne Fondue Fest

Proof, if any were needed, that neutrals can melt more than gold fillings. Twelve tonnes (metric) of Emmental, a small white wine lake and a barrel of Kirsch combine to make this Europe's cheesiest get-together.

EURO-CULTURE

LEGENDARY POETS
Flem Lemming

It is hard to think of Belgian Potato Poetry without the words 'dreadful' and possibly 'starchy' springing to mind. To qualify for membership of the Royal Belgian Root Vegetable Hall of Fame, candidates must wear nothing but potato skins and spend a January night in a field of weevil-resistant King Baudouin Pinks. Fleur Lemming achieved the distinction at his fourth attempt after having his jaws wired up to prevent him eating the potato skins or 'jacket jacket'.

> *Beneath the mud of Flanders*
> *Or what some call the earth*
> *Of what the French call* pommes de terre
> *You'll find we have no dearth*
>
> *We cut them up in various ways*
> *Some wide, some fat, some thinner*
> *Then we make some mayonnaise*
> *And have them for our dinner*

EUROCON – THE EUROPEAN CONSTITUTION

If we've been good boys and girls, Nanny has said we can stay up late and vote in a referendum on the European Constitution. Lucky us. Just in case you haven't been paying close attention to this ludicrous foothill of the European Paper Mountain, here is a summary:

Article 1

Europe will have a president, who will be known as the President of Europe. He or she, unless of transgenderal orientation, must be over fifteen years of age and will be able to call upon the services of a fleet of black, bomb-proof BMWs with windows that can darken at the flick of a switch.

Article 2

Within the enlarged community of twenty-five nations and counting, nobody shall work for more than twenty-two hours in any week or period of seven days, including travelling and toileting time.

Article 3

Article 3 is unavailable at this point owing to an impasse involving the translation into Flemish of the phrase 'boredom threshold'.

Article 4

All Europeans must work together, striving harmoniously and without discrimination towards a common goal of mutually achieved and sustainable fulfilment.

Article 5

All policies of defence, foreign affairs, taxation, justice, trade etc. will be decided by ~~the French and the Germans~~ Brussels.

HOW TO VOTE ON THE EUROPEAN CONSTITUTION

T o help you reach a sensible and informed decision on how to vote in the forthcoming European Constitution referendum we are taking the unusual step of showing you the ballot paper in advance. So here it is …

European Constitution Referendum

Tick only one box

I wish to go back to the Middle Ages and endure isolation, penury, famine and plague. ☐

I'm not too bothered one way or the other. ☐

But seriously folks, at the time of writing it seems that ten countries are going to be holding referendums on the European Constitution. If some of these countries vote 'No', the whole thing comes tumbling down which is why it wasn't quite so brave of T Blair Esq. to announce the British referendum. Chances are it will be cancelled because someone else – and it might even be France – will have stuck their oar in first.

HEROES OF EUROPE

Bernhardt Ruhlbender
1440–1514

The Austrian patriot and tax collector, known by some as the father of VAT. In 1492, in the same week that Christopher Columbus 'discovered' America, Bernhardt issued his first invoice. It was a one-schilling demand for his neighbour, Frau Stoolicker, to cough up for calf-fattening services rendered by her neighbour. When she refused to pay, Bernhardt had her horse-whipped then crucified, quite typical punishments for the time, except that Frau Stoolicker was his mother.

A GUIDE TO
FOREIGN PARTS

Portugal

Portugal is very much a latecomer to what we historians refer to as 'The Twentieth-First Century'. This is not really surprising when you consider that for forty-odd years one man, a complete swine called Dr Antonio Salazar, was allowed to remain in charge. Portugal's main problem was that it once owned large chunks of Africa, which it regarded as 'inalienable'. In the mid-1970s, after a decade of the most intense colony-bashing, Lisbon finally came to terms with the fact that it was in charge of nothing more than itself, the Azores and the cake-rich island of Madeira.

A DAY IN THE LIFE OF LISBON

All Saints Day, 1 November 1755, was a good day to give Lisbon a wide berth and head well inland. In the morning there were three massive earthquakes, felt over much of Europe and North Africa. Then stranger things began to happen ... the sea drained from Lisbon harbour and crowds gathered to root around for sunken objects and coins. Then an eighty-foot-high tidal wave came along – presumably causing more objects to sink. So remember, if you're sipping a port and lemon down by Lisbon harbour and the tide goes out unexpectedly after a huge earthquake: blow up your lilo and head for the hills.

DENMARK: *Coming up in ten pages ... probably.*

HEROES OF EUROPE

Benjy Palme
1482–1537

Glove-maker to Eric IV of Sweden and the man who single-handedly lifted European glove-making out of the mitten-bound Middle Ages. Little is known about Benjy, other than tales of his incredible manual dexterity – he could sew two garments simultaneously, one in each hand. But for one exploit he will forever remain a legend to the people of Sweden – the pitch-black November evening in the forest of Trollsen when he removed a splinter from King Eric's personal earwig.

ALBANIAN SURPRISE

It's not every day that a bold new art form walks up and smacks you on the nose. Let me explain: for decades it was assumed that the interminable output of the Albanian Peasant Poets Collective was about as artistically valid as the instructions on a tin of macaroni cheese. Now, thanks to the painstaking research of Dr Emily Snelgrove, we are amazed to learn that throughout Albania's political ice age many of these 'poets' were in fact being highly subversive. Forced to use Stalinist verse structures, they nevertheless infiltrated complex and coded jokes, and, at no small risk to themselves, even contrived to attack the leadership. Here for example is ostensibly one of the most tedious 'poems' ever to have violated an innocent piece of paper …

I strive in every possible way to be the most stalwart
  comrade of the proletariat
Wanting no finer expression of their perfection
  than the leader of our dynamic secretariat

To whom the proudly independent people of
   Albania make this appeal
Hold us close to your bosom that we may feel
   your revolutionary zeal
Your uniquely correct vision is our only hope
Hand me please your enemies and a good length of
   rope

Oh deary me, poetry's answer to a bowl of All Bran, you might well think – but wait. Look again ... look deeper, remark if you will the first word of each line. Aha, do we not detect the influence of early Lennon and McCartney? Brave bard, I salute you sir, in fact, I want to hold your hand.

EUROPE ON
$500,000 A DAY

Half a million dollars obviously doesn't go as far as it used to. However, I can see no overpowering reason why a chap shouldn't be able to keep himself in wine and roses on such a budget, as well as afford himself a reasonable degree of insulation from the barbarities of the Continent.

Let us start our day at London's Heathrow Airport with a few stiffeners in the Concorde lounge. Meanwhile our Falcon 900 execu-jet is being readied for a full-fuel take-off, thus keeping all options open. Remember, you might not like it when you get there. (Up until recently there was nothing to stop you hiring Concorde itself of course, a snip at £40,000 per flying hour. The problem is that the French were given the job of making the exhaust pipes, so there were very few countries that would tolerate the noise.)

Where to go? This is the big question … up to the Arctic Circle? Down to the Med? Across to the

Muslim Republics of the former Soviet Union? Europe is our oyster, let us prise it open and suck up its fleshy parts. Our pilot for the day, Squadron Leader 'Gin' Ginger. He looks a decent sort, let's see if he's got a tip. 'Keep in the air old boy, that's my advice. Freddie

Foreigner – never had any time for him unless I could see him through a bombsight.'

THE SCHEDULE

9.45 Abandon UK terra firma. Set course for Stavanger, Norway.

10.10 Induce pilot to buzz a couple of North Sea oil platforms.

10.12 Receive severe ticking off from Norwegian air traffic control. Write out one hundred times: 'I must not fly between the legs.'

11.08 Intercepted by two spanking new, K-reg SAAB Grippen fighters of the Swedish Air Force. Wave bottle of aquavit at pilots. They peel off … their flying suits and flash tits.

11.51 Evacuate on-board loos over Elysee Palace. Continue south. According to the on-board masseuse, there are some wicked boutiques if we head over the border into a place called Italy.

12.33 Touch down at Milan's Lambretta Airport. Decamp into Fiat Super Trafficanti saloon and make our way to the establishment of a Mr Giorgio Armanaleggi, purveyor of strides and smells to the financially unassailable. Pleasant enough fellow – threw in a pair of platinum nostril-hair tweakers.

1.00 Lunch. There is, as you can imagine, a fair bit of discussion as to our luncheon requirements. 'I know,' says Ginger, 'we can eat where the President eats.' 'Oh you're fond of prison food are you?' I quip. At length we settle on the idea of a bite on the island of Capri, at an unassuming little place once frequented by the Emperor Tiberius. I don't propose to bore you with the *à la carte* description. Suffice it to say that the *brochette* of Caspian sturgeon, served not on porcelain or ivory, but within the ripening cleavage of a comely slave girl, is entirely toothsome.

4.10 Touchdown at Rome's Cornetto Airstrip, where we are met by no less a vehicle than the Popemobile. Wrongfoot paparazzi by slipping into a side door of the Vatican, where we are warmly greeted by the Vicar of Rome, his Holiness John Paul II. 'Call me J.P.,' he says. And would you do me the honour of letting me mark your game this afternoon?' Perhaps I should explain … The incomparable David Bryant MBE, the winner of the English Out-door Bowls title in the year of my birth and a formidable presence on any bowling green ever since, is among our company.

England has given much to the world – Shakespeare, parliamentary democracy, a decent home for the Elgin Marbles – but I believe our greatest gift is that most civilizing influence: the game of bowls. Here is the game's greatest ambassador, who it has been my lifelong ambition to challenge, and I know that the Pontiff has a small private garden ideally suited to the purpose. And now, the man who has God on his side is about to mark our match!

'Would you care to see the Sistine Chapel before you start?' asks the Pope.

'I think we'll get in a few trial ends if you don't mind,' I reply.

Here may not be the best place for the blow-by-blow account that such a game deserves. The essential facts are contained in a special edition of *The Bowler's Gazeteer*, April '94, from which Norman Mailer is currently writing a screenplay with the working title *Holy Rollers*. Be satisfied if I tell you that, after the match, David Bryant MBE flung himself upon the green and begged for one of the Swiss guards to cut off his arms with a halberd.

Had not his Holiness interceded with disarming haste, English culture might well have been dealt a mortal blow.

8.15 Having whispered the Third Secret of Fatima in my ear, J.P. takes his leave. President and Mrs Bush have been kept waiting long enough. As the sun sets along the Appian Way, the Falcon soars west. Our goal – Lisbon, there to perform a sacred papal mission. Ginger is drinking oxygenated holy water but we have our misgivings about his fondling of the autopilot.

9.52 Disembark at Aeropunto Lisbono where Cardinal Schoonero, formerly the Primate of Angola, is there to greet us. 'Thank heavens you're here,' he cries. 'Come quickly, we have no time to lose.' Shortly after ten o'clock our motorcade crashes through the doors of a dingy warehouse. Inside, lit by a single hurricane lamp, is a scene of pre-industrial squalor, of human suffering the like of which I would gladly not witness again. Children, nine and ten years old, are everywhere – ragged, bleary-eyed automatons engaged in the manufacture of shoes. Despite their occupation, many are barefoot.

A burly man approaches, enquiring as to the nature of our business. 'Our business is to put you out of business,' I tell him. 'Go now and spread the word throughout this miserable city that child labour will cease immediately.'

'And if I don't?'

'Then you,' puts in the Cardinal, 'or anybody who disobeys will first be excommunicated and then tortured by the Inquisition.'

The swarthy slave-driver trots off and we form the children into an orderly queue. Having enquired as to their rates of remuneration, we then give them one year's salary and two pairs of shoes apiece. Further monies are entrusted to the Cardinal for distribution throughout the rest of Lisbon.

10.48 I must confess to feeling a little weary as we take to the skies once more on the penultimate leg of our Euro-day. A light supper is served of wild fowl, mutton and Cox's

Orange Pippins, washed down with a jug or two of Old Ambridge Royal Separation Ale.

11.51 Descend upon Nice's Aeroport Suppositoire, from where we are thankfully whisked by motor launch to the harbour of Monte Carlo. I head straight up the handsome staircase of the Casino into the Salon Sans Limites where I place my last $15,000 on 26 red. Prince Rainier, who is exercising his feudal right to spin the last wheel of the day, appears somewhat discouraged as the silver ball comes to rest. '*Merde. Mille fois je dis MERDE,*' he screams. Armed with our wages for the following day, we say our goodbyes and return to the friendly fuselage of the Falcon.

The schedule outlined above would obviously not be to everyone's taste. Below are a few suggestions to help you write a timetable for your own $500,000 Euro-day.

- Plate-smashing at the Meissen factory in Thuringia, Germany.
- Yogic flying in Switzerland.
- Freelance bungy-jumping from the Leaning Tower of Pisa.
- Hiring the Acropolis and the Athens Symphony Orchestra to play you the theme from *Inspector Morse*.
- A quick half-hour at the Perigourd truffle auctions.
- Lounging at home and listening to *Test Match Special*.

EURO-CULTURE

LEGENDARY POETS
Giuseppe Lambrettini

I'm sure we all acknowledge the debt owed by poetry to the Mediterranean. Expunge the briny from Homer of Virgil, imagine no salty moisture within the pages of Masefield and Byron – to me it does not bear thinking about. In Sicily, at least, the maritime tradition remains joyously alive thanks to the genius of Lambrettini.

> *Between land and sea*
> *Is the beach I comb*
> *My hair into a quiff*
> *The crested waves*
> *On the topless shore*
> *Break over the bows of my skiff*
>
> *Two suntanned breasts*
> *Come floating by*
> *I press upon my oar*
> *Yorkshire girls are easy*
> *But I wish they wouldn't snore*

DOUBLE DANISH

Ask for a bookshop in Copenhagen and you'll be directed to the 'boghandel'. Should it happen to have a lift, you may well find yourself confronted by the words 'I Fart', but this won't surprise you because you've only that minute purchased a timetable, otherwise known as a 'Fartplan'. Later in the day perhaps you'll be relaxing in a foam bath with a beautiful girl. In reality of course, you'll be lying in a 'scum-bad' with a 'smuk pige', but you'll get clean anyway … probably.

HEROES OF EUROPE

Colonel Otto Von Fetisch
1784–1841

The inventor of the jackboot. Prussia's answer to the Duke of Wellington was sent away to boarding school at the age of four, where he developed a taste for monocles and Battenburg cake, neither of which he was permitted to indulge in. Twice during the holidays he ran back to school complaining of soft treatment and 'too much glass in the windows'. Once, when being given a severe kicking by some older boys, Otto was heard to remark, 'Is *das* the best you can do? What are you afraid of – spoiling your shoes?' 'Well, yes, as a matter of fact, we are,' replied his tormentors.

Otto, still only seven, went without sleep for three months and, working by the flame of a single candle, proceeded to re-engineer the military boot as it then existed. While testing an early prototype, he contrived to break both his ankles when clicking his heels together, but failure was unimaginable.

THE BACK-TO-BASICS GUIDE TO SEX-CRAZED EUROPE

AN INDUSTRIALIST'S VIEW

Isn't sex disgusting? Personally I think there's a great deal too much of it in this country, but when I travel on the Continent I am APPALLED by the extent to which it is shamelessly practised and indeed paraded. Hand-holding I have no quibble with, provided it occurs at the appropriate time, i.e. after dark. But, frankly, when I see a mixed team of healthy young Eastern European gymnasts remove their outer garments, rub lubricants on to one another's engorged organs and then disport themselves with two giraffes and some very unusual steel tubing, I start to look for the door.

Take the city of Amsterdam which, I propose, should be twinned with Sodom. The form there seems to be to 'hang out' in a coffee shop while they ply you with drugged cigarettes, then to wander down to an area known as the 'red light district' where, with no warning, you suddenly find yourself confronted by

windows full of scantily clad human flesh. Gigantic breasts, thighs, buttocks and much of it, I am informed, for sale to the highest bidder!

Pity the upright businessman, away on a long trip and exposed to such temptations. Imagine trying to practise your calling as a window-cleaner under these circumstances. And the filth doesn't stop there. I scarcely know how to put this but, believe it or not, it is not merely between Man and Woman that much of this debauchery occurs. I know for a fact that human beings of the SAME gender actually indulge in jiggery-pokery within the city limits of Amsterdam. Worse still, men and women also fall victim to their carnal urges on a SOLITARY basis. No wonder the economy throughout the aptly named 'Low Countries' is run in such a feeble and short-sighted manner.

STOP PRESS – NEW PERVERSION ...
Baby-Sitting Service for Adults

Apparently for 750 euros you can get two nannies to turn up, cook you fish fingers and fruity yogurt, bathe you and get you into your jim-jams then, if you've been good you get a bedtime story.
If you've been naughty it's another 750 euros.

Italy is another sin-infested society where the businessman is strongly advised to travel at all times with a thermos of ice cubes. In Rome and Milan he will continually be finding himself forced to rub up against the most strenuously physical Brazilian transvestites, dazzling beauties every one. I sometimes think that if the Emperor Nero were to reappear and call for public orgies on all the main streets of Rome, the moral climate would if anything improve.

Germany, despite the great strength of its heavy industry, has also alas fallen prey to the hussy and the pornographer. The flesh-pots of Hamburg, many with subdued lighting, permit the sale of alcohol to their patrons, knowing full well that this may encourage the unleashing of bestial urges. More sinister than this, however, is the regular chartering of air transport from German cities to the sweltering kingdom of Thailand. Here, under the pretext of receiving a therapeutic massage, young men are often trapped into sordid sexual encounters with as many as three highly attractive hostesses!

Portugal has the dubious distinction of being the European country where women are most likely to have been anally violated. Why they should demand satisfaction in this unnatural manner is quite beyond me, but here's a tip for the business traveller. If you offer your seat on the bus to a comely Miss from Lisbon, don't be surprised if she doesn't accept. The poor girl's probably dying to sit down. The problem is, she can't.

THE CANNABIS CUP

Amsterdam's answer to the Chelsea Flower Show is the Cannabis Cup, an annual flowering of hydroponic husbandry which sees dedicated potheads making the pilgrimage from as far afield as Penzance and Paraguay. (By the way, if you've ever wondered why there is a small but significantly stoned Paraguayan community gorging themselves on clotted cream in our nation's western extremities and why, along the estuary of the River Plate, scones in lobster pots are sometimes offered for sale, you need be puzzled no more.)

Here for your edification is a selection of Category Winners for the 2005 finals:

Best New Cross-strain
Resin Ruudi's sub-orbital Puberty Reverser

Strongest Variety
Old Van Dyke's Rotterdam Lobotomiser

Best Newcomer
Queen Juliana's Red Light Reserve

Le Palme Vert
Maastricht Midnight Mind Fucker

Prizes were awarded by the Dutch Under Secretary for Soft Drugs, Cornelius van Higher, who had this to say ...

"My fellow tokers and voters, I have already spoken for too long and smoked far too little, or is it the other way round? Who am I to stand here naked before you wasting your valuable time when the whole nation demands Growth? Well I'll tell you who I am ... I am the sister of Jimi Hendrix and you can call me Mimi. Boy could I use a strong cup of coffee."

A GUIDE TO
FOREIGN PARTS

Switzerland

Probably the most boring country in the northern hemisphere, let alone Europe. The main amusement of the citizens of Geneva, apart from supplying nerve gas and small arms to the world's dictators, is watching the crestfallen expressions of tourists rash enough to order a whole cup of coffee. The Swiss franc is Europe's most stable currency for two reasons: very few non-Swiss can afford them and those that can keep forgetting the numbers of their secret bank accounts.

Given apples and motion, the English produced Isaac Newton, the Swiss William Tell.

A GUIDE TO
FOREIGN PARTS

The Czech Republic

What do the composers Dvořák and Janáček, the tennis players Ivan Lendl and Martina Navratilova, the *Hello!*-adorning Ivana Trump and the late (with payment) Robert Maxwell have in common, apart from being Czech? They were all involved in some kind of racket.

Czechs have been known for centuries for their golden hands; for their skill as silversmiths, glass-makers, musicians and craftsmen of all persuasions. Let us therefore look at a typical day in the life of a typical Bohemian resident of Prague.

7.00 am ceremonial washing of the hands.

8.00 am clasp hands together in prayer in Prague's main cathedral, St Vitus (no dancing please).

10.00 am run off a pair of fabulous earrings back at the workshop.

12.00 am lunch. Czechs are not exactly Europe's leading weight-watchers and this is why. They are hopelessly addicted to dumplings, which they raise to their lips along with sour cabbage and roast pork. On the side may well be a bowl of tripe soup, the four-stomach variety being especially favoured. Regular manual exercise is encouraged throughout the luncheon period by the lifting of giant glasses of beer.

3.00 pm more ceremonial hand-washing.

4.00 pm a couple of sets of tennis to help work off lunch. Note, the nets on all Prague's public tennis courts are reinforced with carbon fibre because any Czech teenager worth his or her salt delivers the ball at well over 100 mph even on their second service.

6.00 pm off to a constitutional conference to help re-draw the map. The 'velvet divorce' resulted in the formation of Slovakia and the Czech Republic. Close to the border, you will actually find the town of Dvorce, where negotiations were frequently held.

9.00 pm after a quick dumpling burry or two, most Bohemians will wander down to one of the large roundabouts on the outskirts of Prague. Here they will politely mis-direct the hordes of East Germans who are currently plaguing the country in search of cut-price beer and dumplings.

10.30 pm glove puppetry, finger-painting, a visit to one of the city's 4,000 manicurists and a final ceremonial handwash.

POLISH COAL POETRY

For almost fifty years Polish poetry was forced, literally, underground. As Poles have always written about what they could see and touch, the results have often been dismissed as dark, lumpen and unyielding. But don't please slag it off as a fossilized genre – not until you've experienced the raw realism and carbonated fury of this.

> *Coal*
> *You bastard*
> *Up my nose*
> *In my eyes and teeth*
> *Making it hard for me*
> *To scratch there lines upon your face*
> *Watch out*
> *Here comes Grigor the Grass*
> *Why don't you collapse on him*
> *And we can pull him free*
> *By his testicles*
>
> Anon.

EUROPE GOES TO WAR

If there is one pastime to which Europeans appear hopelessly addicted, it is killing each other. The Seven Weeks' War, the Seven Years' War, the Thirty Years' War and, yes, the Hundred Years' War. Every centimetre of Europe must by now have been trampled by the feet of infantrymen or the hooves of the Heavy Brigade. If you were a (former) Soviet general trying to decide whether to lob over a strategic or a battlefield nuclear weapon, you'd have a really hard decision. The whole place is one gigantic battlefield. More blood has fallen on European soil than rain over the past few centuries.

Why is it that when we think of war we think of Germans? Because they're always starting them. True. Another reason is the large number of Germans who have developed philosophical theories on the subject – otherwise known as excuses for invading their neighbours. According to the philosopher Friedrich Hegel (1770–1831), war is a manifestation of the moral strength of a state or nation. War strengthens the state

'An army marches on its boots'
FELDMARSCHALL ERWIN SCHWANTZFINDER

and is thus an instrument of moral progress. Another German for whom fighting wars seemed like a splendid idea was Karl von Clausewitz (1780–1831). He regarded war as a normal phase in the relations between states and as a normal instrument of state policy. War needed no moral justification beyond its effectiveness in achieving political goals.

Hegel and von Clausewitz weren't the only Germans to tickle their brains with a bayonet. For his theory of 'Total War' we have one Erich Ludendorff (1865–1937) to thank. From Erich's point of view, 'War helps a nation to survive, awakens its soul and stimulates its will to live. The state must prepare the nation for total war through a mobilization of all resources. It must select the enemy or invent him if he does not exist.'

And there are others, General Karl Haushofer (1869–1946) for example, to whom we are indebted for the concept *of lebensraum* or living space ... 'A great country needs to obtain *lebensraum* in order to ensure economic self-sufficiency and provide for a large growth in population.' Now, that wouldn't be Germany you had in mind there by any chance, would it, Karl?

The Hun has been bleating recently that we Britishers should desist forthwith from further mention of the Second World War. Now, we can all understand how it might be a bit annoying for them to be stereotyped as ruthless, goose-stepping fanatics with no regard for truth or decency, but which, I ask you, is preferable: a few grumpy Germans or another Adolf Schicklgrüber? Lighten up, Fritz.

YURI GALITZINE

I tend to think of Ukrainian poetry as being a little like a chicken Kiev ... relatively mundane at first appearances, but always liable to squirt you in the eye with a blindingly hot shaft of pungency should you probe into its deeper recesses.

> *Our combine harvesters*
> *Cut stalks of corn*
> *On parallel paths*
> *We eat rye bread*
>
> *We are adult*
> *But we did not adulterate the petrol*
> *We spend our roubles*
> *And eat more rye bread ...*
> *Then the shagging begins*

TEN THINGS YOU PROBABLY DIDN'T KNOW ABOUT ADOLF HITLER

Among the many murderous tyrants Europe has produced over the centuries, none was perhaps such a complete swine as Adolf Hitler. Apart from anything else he was responsible for the deaths of a million children.

Leaving aside such matters as the Final Solution, the invasions of numerous other countries and the attempted invasion of Great Britain for goodness sake, let us try and understand *der Fuehrer* a little better.

1 Adolf Hitler failed to obtain his school certificate.

2 He failed twice to gain entry to the Vienna Academy of Fine Arts and because he didn't have his school certificate they wouldn't let him into architecture school either.

3 Hitler was a lazy sod. Once in a position of power

he tended to rise late, have a rant or two, take a lengthy siesta and then spend most of his evenings watching trashy films.

4 Although he didn't use alcohol, in terms of drug consumption Hitler was the Elvis Presley of dictators.

5 To celebrate the invasion of Russia (Operation Barbarossa), Hitler, a vegetarian himself, gave his favourite Alsatian (dog) chicken Kiev.

6 Despite sending countless thousand 'degenerate' homosexuals to their deaths, Hitler himself was a raging poof. If you don't believe me, read *The Hidden Hitler* by Lothar Machtan, Perseus Press 2001. Before, during and after the First World War, Adolf had numerous gay liaisons. Some of his boyfriends received cushy jobs and pensions to buy their silence, others were murdered to maintain the superhuman reputation of the Fuehrer.

The Commandant of Landsberg prison where Adolf, Hess and others were held after an abortive 1923 coup was obliged to order his Nazi charges, 'not to practise nudity outside their own section of the prison'.

7 In his early days, to convey an impression of forcefulness, Hitler always used to carry a heavy riding whip made of hippopotamus hide.

8 In 1909 Hitler's half-brother Alois was working as a

waiter in Dublin. Alois eloped with Bridget, a local lass and in due course William Patrick Hitler entered the world. According to Bridget, when the child was about two, Uncle Adolf came to stay with them in London in order to avoid being called up for Austrian military service. Bridget it was who advised the young man to trim his handlebar moustache into the more widely recognized toothbrush design. William Patrick Hitler went on to spend time in Germany and serve in the US Navy. He raised a family and lived in Long Island for over fifty years.

9 Hitler loathed Charlie Chaplin even before *The Great Dictator* appeared. Chaplin visited Berlin in 1931 and drew massive crowds. After the visit the SS found evidence of Chaplin's Jewish ancestry, which was duly splashed across the papers. Chaplin had no Jewish ancestry.

10 Right up to his ignominious end, Hitler was furiously developing new secret or 'revenge' weapons to turn the tide of the war. Among those in the pipeline were the nuclear bomb, the Amerika bomber and the V3 and V4.

EURO-CULTURE

LEGENDARY POETS
Ouzo Bouzouki

The Homeric tradition lives on! Man struggling against the elements, the gods, or, in this case, the bottle. The hangover Poets of Paxos take their calling seriously, none more so than Ouzo Bouzouki.

I will kill Stavros
As soon as I can walk
Which
I trust
Will be shortly after
I am able to see

Oh why did I drink his retsina
My brain feels like warm semolina
My bowels are the roost of a squadron of owls
I should have had lavatory cleaner

JOHN BULL'S EUROQUIZ

It is important to know exactly what you're up against when you set foot in Europe or – and this is becoming increasingly common – when Europe decides to set foot over here. Already much of our water supply is in French control, many of the vehicles on our roads are of German construction and ever-greater numbers of dentists' waiting rooms contain copies of the pitiful Spanish trash-sheet, *Hello!* magazine. You need to be razor-sharp these days, so hone your wits on my Euro-questions and the Best of British to you.

GEOGRAPHY

1 What are the capitals of these mighty world powers?
   a) Liechtenstein
   b) Andorra
   c) San Marino
   d) Monaco

2 Why is the 2006 World Cup to be held in Germany?

3 In which countries are these rude places?
   a) Assing
   b) Ballstadt
   c) Cunihat
   d) Mt Penice
   e) Wankendorf

4 Why does Roger Moore live in Switzerland?

5 Was it recently illegal in Albania to:
   a) Grow a beard
   b) Wear flared trousers
   c) Listen to, make or broadcast pop music
   d) Export the Lek (the local and virtually worthless currency)

LITERATURE

6 Which of these books has made the greatest contribution to the life of the intellect and the furtherance of European culture?
   a) *Don Quixote* Cervantes
   b) *The Decameron* Boccaccio
   c) *Les Misérables* Hugo
   d) *The Trial* Kafka
   e) *The Magic Mountain* Mann

f) *The I Hate the French Official Handbook*
Thatcher & Scott

POLITICS

7 How many assassination attempts were made on General de Gaulle?
   a) 4
   b) 31
   c) Not enough

8 Why does Bernhard Langer wear two pairs of underpants?

9 How many of Italy's 630 deputies have 1: been investigated for links with the Mafia? 2: starred in porno movies? 3: are related to Benito Mussolini?
   a) 1
   b) 305
   c) all of them

10 If Portugal is Britain's oldest ally, why aren't they friendlier now?

11 What is the difference between a feta cheese and wet cardboard?

12 Count Lajos Bathyany is remembered in Hungary as the martyr to scrupulous loyalty. Sentenced to

death by hanging, he slit his own throat with a knife smuggled to him inside a loaf of bread. But how did he actually die?

ANSWERS: 1 a) Vaduz b) Andorra La Vella c) San Marino d) Monaco-ville; 2 To give them a slim chance of getting past the first round; 3 a) Denmark b) Germany c) France d) Italy e) Germany; 4 To avoid paying tax; 5 Sorry – for reasons of state security I can't answer this one; 6 – an easy one – f; 7 c; 8 In case he gets a hole in one; 9 I wouldn't answer this question if I were you; 10 You tell me!; 11 Not a lot; 12 He was shot.

A GUIDE TO
FOREIGN PARTS

Scandinavia

I am not among those who believe that Her Majesty's Government should charge or tax the Scandinavians for the privilege of receiving fine British acid rain. Rather, like the BBC World Service, it should be freely bestowed regardless of race, creed or degree of barbarity.

And, make no mistake, despite their outward veneer of sophistication, few peoples are as unutterably and incorrigibly barbaric as the Nord and the Viking. Let's get down to the facts – the Saab Viggen fighter is the only military jet to have central locking and electric windows; Björn Borg's eyes are so close together that he cannot use binoculars; and were it not for the inexplicable popularity of Abba, Sweden would long ago have called in the receivers, bankrupted by its 'herrings for all' welfare state. Swedes choose to lounge around in super-heated wooden cabins, absorbing one

another's excess body fluids, chiefly aquavit. Norway is where men are Men and the elk are nervous.

Scandinavia has no history to speak of, merely the passage of a few blood-loving cretins across an immense frozen wilderness. Stockholm means literally

'Big Snowball' and was where, in the ninth century, Ik and his son Iksen once put up a large igloo. Unfortunately, this architectural marvel was erected on an ice floe in Stockholm harbour and father and son were soon melting their way across the Baltic.

> *Speculation is that the Swedes are slowly boring themselves to death. This is certainly the case if their cars and movies are any indication*
>
> P J O'ROURKE

50

FIRST-CLASS
REASONS TO HATE
EUROPE

—Part Three—

21 Rabies

22 Bouzouki music

23 Bureaux de change

24 The European Commission (of massive
   fraud upon the British tax-payer)

25 Oompah bands

26 Yodelling

27 Euro-passports

28 Kinder Surprise

29 Cyprus

30 Lederhosen

EURO-MONEY

If Europe is about anything at all, and there are many of us who feel it isn't, it is about MONEY. It is about fat bankers* wanting more of the stuff having four-hour lunches with the tubby politicians who print it. Now, where do these bankers see their next little earner coming from? How will their wallets remain snugly lined in the years to come? The answer, in a word is 'expansion'.

It may not have escaped your notice that Europe contains a lot of very poor people, many of whom have the misfortune to live in places like Poland. Quite understandably, many of these financially challenged individuals would like to drive BMWs and buy their boxer shorts in Harrods. But how could this ever be?

* When I say 'fat bankers', I refer really to the whole caboodle of pocket-lining middle men, i.e. fat stockbrokers, speculators, fixers, lawyers, fund managers, foreign exchange dealers, shysters, accountants, ad-men etc., i.e. those whose business is to create wealth – principally their own.

How can a poor, Polish peasant hope to take out a subscription to *Penthouse*? The answer, in a word, is 'borrow'. And who do people tend to borrow from? You've got it – bankers.

Generally speaking, the poorer you are, the more the banker stands to gain. Should you happen to be starving and desperate, a complete stitch-up is pretty much odds-on. Don't forget that bankers have had decades of practice swindling Africans and South Americans.

From the bankers' point of view there is more to interest than mere interest. There are whacking great consultancy and privatization fees to be 'earned'. They can take equity stakes in property and industrial developments. They gain access to cheap labour; perhaps some attractively priced raw materials. The opportunities for exploiting Europe's former communist dictatorships are limited only by the bankers' imagination and greed – and they are unimaginably greedy. And, should they actually succeed in enriching any of their client nations, no one is better placed to help them spend their newfound wealth (on BMWs, satellite dishes and soft lavatory paper) than the fat banker – for a fat fee, of course (plus lunch and a Euro-hooker).

INTERESTING BELGIANS

NUMBER 2
Ritchard Jorgnbilder

Just off the Grand'Place in Brussels, amongst the restaurants of the Marche des Herbes, you can find the tiny cheese shop 'Le Souffle' owned and run since 1963 by Ritchard Jorgnbilder.

Ritchard is an expert on the aromatic cheeses of Europe, as you can tell as soon as you get within a hundred yards of his establishment. The smells of wet goat and French *pissoir* draw in his loyal customers as efficiently as they deflect the untrained cheese-hunter.

We spoke to him in the shop after he had locked away some of the stronger examples in his air-tight storage room. We asked him to name some of his favourite cheeses.

He insisted on us first trying his local favourite, *Remoudou*. This is called the 'Stinking Cheese' – with good reason. But once our eyes stopped watering, we found that this 7 oz loaf cheese with its brownish-orange rind was very rich and tasty. Then he dragged out a 15 lb drum of *Freise Nagelkaas*, 'Nail Cheese' from the North of Holland. The spicy coating of cloves and cumin seeds was agreeable enough but the hard, grey, dry interior could well have been used to build a table.

Swiss Sapsago, on the other hand, would make excellent building stone. The unusual smell, strong flavour and pale-green colour come from Blue Melilot, a Middle Eastern herb. The cheese must first be grated with the aid of a special device which would probably be very useful for removing dead skin from the soles of the elderly.

Finally, now our tastebuds had been well and truly whetted, Ritchard showed us two Spanish cheeses. *Gamonedo* is a seriously smelly mixed-milk cheese from the mountains of Asturias where it is used to keep the mosquitoes away. *Quesos Anejo de Cabra de la Sierra de Huelva*, despite being made from goat's milk, is no different – it just has a stupid name.

We left Mr Jorgnbilder's unique emporium, our minds buzzing with recondite information, our hearts full of admiration for this passionate advocate of the curd and the whey – and our stomachs churning. Fortunately, a prudent short-term insurance policy covered the emergency flight home and the subsequent fortnight in the Partridge Place Nursing Home for the Intestinally Disadvantaged.

A GUIDE TO
FOREIGN PARTS

France

It is not the authors' intention to dwell unduly amongst the unwashed and untrustworthy citizens of Gaul. We have dealt with them already in a companion volume, *The I Hate the French Official Handbook*, and fear not, their dubious practices are being vigilantly monitored for the surely-to-be-published *The I Still Hate the French Official Handbook*.

Suffice it to say that France continues to top the table of European nations who flout European law. Their economy is in freefall, their sybaritic president staggers from one scandal to the next and they still charge the British motorist for tap water at their 'service' stations.

When French astronaut Colonel Jean-Loup Chrétien joined Soviet cosmonauts on a joint mission in 1982, he was well supplied. A series of special space gourmet meals was prepared for him, including jugged hare,

crab soup, and lobster pilaf with sauce a l'Armoricaine. This heavy food was designed to test the reactions of the body's cardiovascular systems during the flight – well, that was the excuse anyway.

The worst xenophobes on earth are the French, a nation protected by a cloud of garlic breath which still built the Maginot Line to keep foreigners out. Chauvinism is a French word which cannot even be translated, so Froggie is the emotion it describes.

NATIONAL LAMPOON

THE EUROPEAN (WASTE OF) SPACE AGENCY

As if messing up this planet wasn't enough, Europe has seen fit to poke its inky little finger into the heavens. On 17 September 2004, at vast expense, an Ariane 5 rocket was launched carrying the catchily named Sloshat-FLEVO experiment.

Shaped like a cube, Sloshat-FLEVO weighs 129 kilograms and contains 33.5 litres of de-ionised water in a special tank. As the water sloshes about (hence the name Sloshat), 270 sensors will measure the water's distribution. Other sensors will record temperature, pressure and fluid velocity at seventeen locations. According to the European Space Agency's website, this is the first time a satellite has been dedicated to studying fluid behaviour in weightlessness. According to me, Europe is breaking new ground in the field of pointlessness.

EUROZONE LAYER'S GOT A HOLE IN IT, MATE

The ESA employs 2,000 staff and is based in Paris. The budget is astronomical, but then space exploration is all about vanity and prestige and nobody is vainer or more in need of a boost than the French. Jules Verne has a lot to answer for.

The author of *20,000 Leagues Under the Bidet* was supposed to have been a lawyer, but at college his imagination ran riot, as did his libido by all accounts. He yearned to travel – up into space, down into the very bowels of the earth, but for me *Around the World with Eighty Suppositories* will always be his masterpiece.

GREAT EUROPEAN CRACKPOTS

NUMBER 4
Werner Herzog 1942–

The German film director who once made a film about building an opera house in the Amazonian jungle, which required the transportation of a full-size steamboat up a hill (*Fitzcarraldo*).

Unlike the rest of the human race, when he says something like, 'I'll eat my hat', he means it. What he actually said was, 'I'll eat my boot' and he did. However, he marinated it in hot oil for twenty-four hours – which could be construed as cheating – before polishing it off with a knife and fork.

EURO-CULTURE

LEGENDARY POETS
Aase Fjordsen

No one perhaps better expresses the chilling urgency of alpinism within the Arctic context than the Tromso-based bard Aase Fjordsen. Nominated a staggering fourteen times for the prestigious All Norway Poetry Chalice, here is one of her best-known 'frozen water' works.

> *Have you ever tried peeing*
> *While you're cross-country skiing?*
> *Icicles can form*
> *In the essence of your being*

THE CHANNEL TUNNEL

'Those whom God hath seen fit to cast asunder let no man join together'

JOHN BULL

It's all very well building a tunnel under the English Channel, if that's what you fancy, but to make it join up with France of all places is quite frankly Not On. What were they thinking? It's already far too easy for people just to breeze in from France, have a decent breakfast and get their teeth fixed. But this ... this means tens of thousands of extra rucksacks on the

London Underground. It wipes out at a stroke our glorious victories at Agincourt, Crécy and Twickenham. It means Invasion, it means … THE END.

CLAUSTROPHOBIA

Far too little has been written about this important subject. Those of us who travel on the London Underground know that in this country we don't squeal, squirm and start shouting 'Mummy' just because we're stuck in a tunnel with the lights off for an hour or two. This is because we are British.

However, you may be amazed to learn that no provision has been made on the Channel Tunnel for the segregation of Britons from panic-prone Italians, hysterical Frenchmen and, worst of all, nervous Norwegians. This is a recipe for mayhem.

NIGHTMARE BENEATH TH

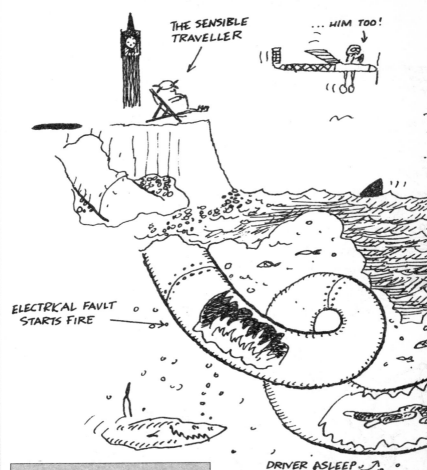

THE SENSIBLE TRAVELLER

... HIM TOO!

ELECTRICAL FAULT STARTS FIRE

DRIVER ASLEEP

UP YOURS APPLE

UNEXPLODED WARTIME BOMBS

HOW TO PLAY

Using the diagram on this page, take turns to imagine all the gruesome ways that you and your family could die while using the Channel Tunnel. Then list them in order of likely unpleasantness.

AVES

EUR BIT
NESE
ATION

TITANIC MARU

AN EAGER
CONTINENTAL
TOURIST

TERRORIST
ATTACHING
LIMPET
MINE

TWO THOUSAND
ARSENAL
SUPPORTERS

BLOODY KRAUT
MINE

EARTHQUAKE

A GUIDE TO
FOREIGN PARTS

Luxembourg

Whoever heard of a crappy pop-music station masquerading as a decision-making nation in the vanguard of international affairs? Occupying a mere 2,600 square kilometres in a topographical crease between Belgium, Germany and France, the Grand Duchy of Fab 208 was one of the six founders of the Common Market in 1957. The guide books say that its unspoilt countryside will 'delight the most indifferent traveller'. Don't kid yourself. Nod off for a second on Eurorail and you'll miss it.

> *On a clear day, from the terrace, you can't see Luxembourg at all. This is because a tree is in the way.*
>
> ALAN COREN

THE WONDERFUL
WORLD OF THE CAP

The EC Common Agricultural Policy (CAP) is a key part of the Common Market set-up. You can tell because it works hard to stop market forces having any real effect. Every time you buy food, about a tenth of the total bill goes to pay European farmers prices in excess of world levels.

CAP IN HAND

In the 1970s, the main argument in favour of the CAP was continuity of supply. How could we trust foreigners, like Australians and Americans, not to cut off our supply of wheat or sugar? We had to be self-sufficient. The EC is now a net exporter (or dumper) of many foodstuffs.

In the 1980s, the case turned to the support of the farming population. How could we allow rural areas to become depressed, while industry was booming throughout Europe? Surveys were produced, showing that thousands of small-holders could barely eke out a living on bread-crusts. More sophisticated surveys showed that most of those small-holders worked on their fields in the evenings and at weekends; during the week they were working their shifts at Volkswagen or Fiat. In England, we would call such 'farms' allotments.

In the 1990s, the protectionists cited the environment as being in need of financial support. If subsidies are reduced, farms will either become huge outdoor factories, with massive machinery and no hedgerows, or overgrown fields full of weeds and shrubs. Sounds as if there could be an ecological balance in the making there.

IF THE CAP FITS

But it is not just that billions of pounds a year are spent to keep the honest farmer in weed-killer and Range Rovers. It has been estimated (in particular by Proffessor Klaus Tiedemann) that at least ten per cent of total CAP expenditure goes on fraud.

There is barely a product that is not fiddled. In northern Europe, where the crimes are professional and international, the CAP is usually referred to as the Criminally recycled Agricultural Policy. Beef is sent out of the EC for an export premium (the money that farmers are paid to dump their products abroad, ruining the Third World's prospects). It is then smuggled back into the EC and exported again for another premium. Or it is declared for export to a high-premium country (some are more worthy than others) and diverted to a low-premium country (with a better market).

DOUBLE DUTCH CAP

Cheese and butter are subject to similar frauds, the idea being to claim export subsidies on products which are not eligible (e.g. pig-fat masquerading as butter) or paid more than once on the same goods.

Some of these export frauds can be very profitable – several prosecuted cases of individual consignments involved overpayments in excess of £10 million. Nice work – for the criminal export agent – but nothing for the farmer.

In other cases, the products may not exist at all. In some parts of Italy, about 300% of the land surface is planted with olive trees, if the records of the oil pressing plants are to be believed. Just the threat of an investigation in one part of Italy caused a 35% fall in subsidy claims, and the closure of several oil mills.

A LOAD OF OLD CAP

It is believed by some experts that almost the whole of the so-called 'wine lake' (the surplus wine sent for distillation – a billion litres a year) is in fact factory-produced from water, sugar, methanol and a few additives. Some of this 'wine' has occasionally leaked on to the market, with a predictable number of fatalities.

Often the extent of the frauds can be seen by looking at international trade statistics. For example, the subsidy and export statistics show that Germany – a country with few obvious paddy-fields – is a major exporter of rice. No one claims to import all this rice from Germany.

TO CAP IT ALL

We should also remember the cost of distributing all this largesse. The CAP is the largest part of the EC budget, so employs towerblocks full of Eurocrats. Indeed, were it not for the CAP and the related regional grants structure, there would be little financial adminstration needed in the EC at all.

Recently the CAP has been through a major overhaul. Farmers are now to be subsidized according to how much land they own, not on what they grow and production will inevitably fall. Almost unbelievably this will occur just as the world's demand for food is beginning to outstrip the supply. Is there life on Mars?

EURO-CULTURE

LEGENDARY POETS
Franz Wolf-Fokker

German poetry has often been dismissed as 'relentless, mechanical and automotive'. For me, however, there is real emotion – albeit of a somewhat brutish nature – in much of Wolf-Fokker's *oeuvre*, as indeed there is to be found among the poems of many who comprise the school of Dusseldorf Direktline Verseschmidts.

> *Burning up the autobahn*
> *In my Bay M Vay*
> *Thinking of a place to stop*
> *For lunch along the way*
>
> *In my boot a video*
> *Produced by Michael Winner*
> *I will put it on you know*
> *When I get home for dinner*
>
> *P.S.*
> *Hitler built the autobahns*
> *Not personally of course*
> *He merely gave the orders*
> *Between the two world wars*

GREAT EUROPEAN CRACKPOTS

NUMBER 5
Leon Meurant

A Belgian steel-worker, who affected the title of Count Vernier de Miraumont, Meurant was driving a Russian countess to Brussels from Paris in 1946. Her naked corpse was discovered by the roadside a few hours later and the police eventually tracked Meurant down in Germany, where he was passing himself off as a gynaecologist. At first the Count confessed to strangling the unfortunate Russian but later came up with a more ingenious account of her death. He claimed that he was really Operative B-17, a Soviet undercover agent, and that his fellow spook, B-15, had concealed himself in the boot of his car and murdered the countess while searching her body for secret information. 'After all,' he pointed out, 'bras and panties are ideal hiding places for microfilm.'

Surprisingly, his tale was not believed and he was sentenced to death.

However, the Count did not go to the guillotine. As is clear, he was an entertaining fellow and by 1952 had become a favourite with the guards in Amiens jail. One day he offered to demonstrate how the Russian NKVD attached silencers. A guard obligingly handed over his pistol and, presto, Meurant and a fellow murderer were able to walk free wearing prison officers' uniforms. The Count was subsequently recaptured while reading a newspaper account of his escape. He complained bitterly that the police never allowed him to finish reading it.

DENMARK: *It is more than possible, in fact highly likely, that more Danishness will shortly be upon us.*

50
FIRST-CLASS
REASONS TO HATE
EUROPE

——Part Four——

A GUIDE TO FOREIGN PARTS

Spain

Spain has always been a hot and oily country where civilization and culture have traditionally found it hard to get on the agenda. True, the swordsmiths of Toledo were once the makers of the world's finest blades, but what did they use them for? Thrusting into the necks of bulls after the poor creatures had been systematically weakened by the more cowardly assault of lance and dart.

In 1588 Spain had the effrontery to attempt an invasion of Great Britain. They came in great floating castles complete with battlements and 'interviewing' dungeons. Their plans were meticulously drawn up – tear down Shakespeare's new Globe Theatre and run up a multi-storey bull-fighting arena. But *paella* was not to become the national dish of this country so easily.

What did Drake make of this cumbersome and inquisitive flotilla? Marmalade. When Sir Francis had finished his end of bowls, he sallied forth, set some of the Spaniards afire and forced the rest to compete in a Round Britain endurance event for which trawling for squid off the Costa Brava had ill-equipped them. *Olé*.

A JEWEL IN THE CROWN

Not all the Iberian peninsula, or for that matter the Mediterranean, can be dismissed as a wasteland of

jerry-built discos perched on a lake of condoms and jellyfish. For there is a jewel in its midst. An oasis of rocky decency defending civilization against the swarthy Spaniard, the Moor, but most pressingly of all, from the G-stringed German. I refer of course to Gibraltar, that brave outpost, that noble sentinel, towering morally over the effluent-rich Med and where tea is served with cold milk.

QUELQUE CHOSE POUR LE WEEKEND?

The condom, sheath, rubber johnnie or French letter has been with us in Europe since the Middle Ages, roughly since syphilis began to put a bit of a question mark over taking off your trousers.

The following is a list of brand names of European condoms. Using your skill and judgment, match the johnnie with the right country. The eagle-eyed among you will notice there are more brands than countries ...

Le Majestique
Il Terminatorri   Holland
Unimil Extra   France
Phuck   Italy
Phallicos Sensitivos   Poland
Stormschloss   Latvia
WillySafe   Switzerland
Ass Bandito   Ireland
El Barbaro   Greece

Bikeshed deluxe	Spain
Matterhorn	Germany
Vesuvio Stupendo	Portugal
Mahogany	Malta
Fjordmeister	Estonia
Lance of St George	Norway
Happenis	Belgium
Moi	Slovenia

Answers below.

Answers: We are unable to supply answers to the above test due to intervention by EUROCOM (The European Condom Commission), who threaten massive fines if we publish 'commercially and sexually sensitive' information. We naturally appealed to EUROCLONC (The European Condom Council) but unfortunately they rubber-stamped the original decision.

GREAT EUROPEAN CRACKPOTS

NUMBER 6
Sylvestre Matuschka

A Hungarian businessman whose chief delight was to cause train crashes. After a failed attempt in Austria in 1931, he managed to derail a train in Hungary in August 1932, injuring seventy-five people. In September came his finest hour: he blew up an express train on a viaduct and twenty-two people were killed as the carriages plummeted off the bridge. Feigning injury, Matuschka pretended to be among the survivors and subsequently sued Hungarian Railways. To their credit, the police established that Matuschka had never been on the express at all and at his house they discovered plans to blow up trains all over Europe. In court the saboteur confessed that train crashes turned him on sexually and blamed a spirit entity called Leo. He was sentenced to hang but the punishment was commuted to life. The Russians released him during the war so that they could make use of his expertise with explosives.

The European rail network is one of the very few continental success stories. European trains are quick, cheap, comfortable and run on time. The long-abused British commuter might be forgiven the odd pang of jealousy as he waits in the rain for his replacement bus, but on reflection he would not swap his rail service for theirs, no sir. European trains are awash with unwashed Europeans; picnicking, gesticulating, speaking and holding impromptu aftershave competitions.

A GUIDE TO FOREIGN PARTS

Holland

A low country full of lesbians and tourists in dirty macs. In a recent attempt to upgrade its sleazy image, Holland teamed up with Barrett's, the well-known Liquorice Allsort manufacturers, and bogged down British high streets with a chain of health food shops. Apart from the porn trade, their other big business is tulips. Bulbs are smoked openly on the streets of Amsterdam.

A GUIDE TO FOREIGN PARTS

Hungary

In the 1930s Hungary enjoyed the premiership of one Béla Imredy. He was the great hope of the nation's bankers, magnates, priests and other respectable anti-Nazis. However, following the Munich Agreement, under which Hungary was handed a slice of Czechoslovakia, Béla turned Nazi overnight.

In support of the second anti-Jewish Law, which he publicized on Christmas Eve 1938, he declared that 'One drop of Jewish blood is enough to infect a man's character and patriotism.' No sooner had he said so than he turned out to have more than one drop himself – a Jewish great-grandmother in his German-Bohemian ancestry. When the Regent of Hungary showed him the relevant document Béla Imredy (but not for this) fainted.

EURO-CULTURE

LEGENDARY POETS
Olaf Blankke

Finnish Log Poetry, borrowing as it does from the Trappist oral tradition, has long been perceived as 'difficult', if not downright impenetrable to mainstream Western sensibilities. In Finnish there are twenty-three words for sap but only one for happiness. For me the suicidal melancholy of the long dark winter of the Finnish soul is caught, like a moose in the headlights, by these words of Olaf Blankke.

In the hollows of a tree
I build a log cabin
To share with woodpeckers
Woodworm and wood alcohol are my other friends
In Mexico you'd find the worm in the bottle

CALLING DENMARK

Hello. Thank you for calling the Danish Multiple Orgasm Information service. I'm afraid that no one can come on the phone just now, although Sonja thinks she'll be able to manage it by the end of the week.

So how do you most enjoy having orgasms? In Denmark we are asking this question all the time and, believe it or not, our organization has collected and verified over 2,500 different ways that people go 'Oooh, yes.' Some of them are pretty weird, although that's not a word we ever use. For example, there's a lady who lives just here in Aarhus who can only have an orgasm if she's talking to a bus conductor. Imagine her distress when they wanted to introduce one-man buses! Fortunately we were able to petition under Denmark's Orgasm Protection Protocol and we soon put a stop to that.

Anyway, enough of this, you're probably bursting to tell us about your latest experience. Wait till you've got your breath back then tell me your details so that Sonja and Hans Christian can respond to your needs. And, remember, you can use as many rude words as you like.

A curious little country is Denmark, suppliers of water-injected bacon to the Great British Breakfast Table and Carlsberg Special Brew to the Great British Park Bench. Gateway to Sweden but rather too close to Germany for my liking and theirs too ... probably.

A GUIDE TO
FOREIGN PARTS

Small Fry

Inside most big European countries there are small ones waiting to get out. But there are also plenty of small places that have managed to escape the clutches of the Frances and Germanys of this world and be their own boss. Liechtenstein, San Marino, The Vatican, Monaco and Andorra, to name but five. Although these countries had a combined population of only 137,766 in 1990, there's nothing to stop any one of them declaring war on the United Kingdom tomorrow. Except, possibly, common sense and the fact that Andorra, the biggest of the five, currently has a defence budget of nil.

I propose to put these 'small men of Europe' under the microscope ...

SAN MARINO
POPULATION 23,676

Perched on the side of a mountain in northern Italy, San Marino has seen fit to divide itself into nine 'Castles', each with its own 'Castle-Captain'. For five years from 1978, San Marino was the only western European country with a communist-led government. It has embassies in two foreign countries, Iceland and the People's Republic of China.

THE VATICAN
POPULATION 830

The Vatican, the Papal State or Holy City, is untroubled by undue left-wing influence. This wholly Roman suburb, about the size of a polo field, has two official languages, Latin and Italian, and one rather large bank, the Insitute par le Opere di Religione or IOR. Following a whiff of scandal (a dense cloud of corruption, actually) in the 1980s involving Roberto Calvi and Blackfriars Bridge, the IOR's assets are believed to be down to the three to four billion dollar mark.

LIECHTENSTEIN
POPULATION 28,877 (INC. 10,218 REGISTERED ALIENS)

The year 1986 was a big one for Liechtenstein. In January the Landtag, Liechtenstein's parliament, was dissolved by Prince Hans-Adam. The cause? A dispute between the two main parties regarding the building of a new museum to house the royal art collection. Later that year, as if to demonstrate that the Royal Wand could swing both ways, women were finally given the vote. Liechtenstein has a police force of fifty-six men and twenty-two auxiliaries. There has been no standing army since 1868. The principal export apart from banking or laundry services is artificial teeth.

MONACO
POPULATION 29,876

The Grimaldi family has been in charge of Monaco since 1297 but things do change there, honestly. In 1962 Prince Rainer agreed to renounce his divine right to rule and in the Eighties Björn Borg moved in, dealing a serious blow to the Monegasque binocular industry. There are three political parties in Monaco but only one of them wins any seats – the one that supports Prince Rainier. True, the *Mouvement d'Union Democratique* (MUD) did pick up one of the eighteen seats in the Assembly in 1963, but since then they haven't found a place to sit at all. Monaco has no agricultural land and the highest population density of any independent state in the world (15,321 per square km).

ANDORRA
POPULATION 54,507 (INC. 15,616 ANDORRANS)

Andorra is a massive duty-free shop high in the Pyrenees whose inhabitants speak Catalan, French and Spanish. A staggering twelve million people visit the place every year, compared to Liechtenstein's modest twelve thousand. The country's only political organization, the Partit Democratic d'Andorra, is technically illegal and, in the 1981 elections to the General Council, it urged its supporters to cast blank votes.

STOP PRESS
New Small Nation Discovered

Incredible though it may seem, a tiny unknown new nation has just emerged, blinking on to the world stage. No bigger than a cricket pitch, the island of Cardiv lying 15 miles south of Corsica was always believed to be uninhabitable. Now we know that for at least 740 years a community of Welsh-speaking cave dwellers has fashioned an existence, living on fish, birds and the odd wreck.

The discovery of the fifty-four islanders only came to light when three of their number drifted on a raft to the Italian mainland and attempted intimacy with an order of Dominican nuns. Plans to issue stamps are well advanced.

AMERICA

The best, some would say the only thing Europe's got going for it, is that it is not America. And who must we thank for standing full square in the path of the crazed juggernaut of MacDonaldization? Why, if it's not our old chums the French.

They've been at it for years mind you, ever since General de Gaulle pulled France out of NATO in 1966. So despite giving America the Statue of Liberty and allowing the excrescence that is EuroDisney to fester on Gallic soil, the French are most definitely Europe's David when it comes to slinging shots across the bows of the Goliath Satan.

Unfortunately for Claude, two factors serve to blunt the thrust of his yankophobia. The first is that most of the 'new' nations of Europe, the ones who were once in the Warsaw Pact, tend to rather like America. After decades of queuing for cabbage and suffering under Soviet rule, who can really blame them? More importantly though, France's mission to defend Europe from those who would pour ketchup over their *filet mignon* is undermined by us, the British.

We'll lap up their trailer-park tomfoolery and guzzle GM apple pie with a triple Enron unleaded Daisy Cutter side salad. Why? Because Winston Churchill's mother was an American and that's how things have always been. We'll extradite our finest terrorists stateside and bend over to Bill Gates because a few fundamentalist Texans have banged their fist on the table and we were too polite to make a fuss.

Following the disastrous re-election of the T-bone-headed Texan, George 'Whoosh I've fired another one' Bush, the rift between Europe and America, betwixt reason and lunacy, grows wider by the hour. The world's only superpower is falling apart and soon the pieces will require picking up and reassembling.

Britain, France, Spain and the Dutch should all dust down their old maps, go to the Army and Navy Stores and prepare for the re-colonization of the New World.

HEROES OF EUROPE

Fettucio Bollocini
1922–

I take my hat off to Fettucio. He is currently under investigation for corruption as head of Connini, the state-controlled Internal Rainforest Commission. (There is no rainforest in Italy.) He is a Lloyd's name. His 64-year-old wife Antonella has just become pregnant courtesy of the Maria Elena Clinic in Rome. He has extensive property interests in Sarajevo, and his tortoise, Rinaldi, has recently been diagnosed as rabid.

But is he down-hearted? No sir, because Fettucio has just been voted Italy's Bum-Pincher of the Year.

EURO-CULTURE

LEGENDARY POETS
Jean-Luc Dogmar

French poetry is generally reckoned to have disappeared up its own backside some time in 1967. This in no way inhibited a whole generation of oyster-loving, Maoist, Eiffel-towering bores from producing dozens of new poetry reviews with names like *Horsemeat Computer* and *Suicide Nappy Liner*. Indeed, more alleged poetry is published in France than in the whole of the rest of Europe.

Standing aside from such crassness is Jean-Luc Dogmar, an electrician by trade who discovered his poetic 'gift' whilst rewiring Jack Lang's aquarium in the Ministry of Culture:

> *Society*
> *Emprisons me*
> *Like a* pain au chocolat
> *I would be a nihilist*
> *But I can't even be bothered*
> *To make a laundry list*
> *Sex*
> *Oven gloves*
> *Infinity*

STRANGE BUT TRUE

During the Greek archaeological survey near Epirus in 1991, field workers unearthed nearly a million plate fragments, but not a single complete specimen. Many theories were put forward and an experiment was even conducted to test the effects of seismic disturbance on buried earthenware and ceramics. Finally it was discovered that the site had once been a Kapheterium where wedding receptions and other parties (with much primitive plate-smashing) were often held.

50

FIRST-CLASS
REASONS TO HATE
EUROPE

——Part Five——

And finally ...

EIGHT EUROPEANS TO KEEP AN EYE ON*

Nicholas Sarkozy
Wildly ambitious French President-in-waiting.

Peter Mandelson
Britain's one and only European Commissioner. No lack of ambition here. Dog-lover.

Roger Moore
Keep an eye on Roger or he'll keep an eye on you. Then he'll raise an eyebrow ...

Michael Schumacher
The Terminator's younger brother. All things are possible.

Arnold Schwarzenegger
He may be the 'Governator' of California but he can't

be President unless they change the law about being born abroad. When this fact penetrates his Austrian skull maybe he'll remember who he is ...

Jeremy Paxman
Can't believe he's going to sit around writing books about fishing when he finally quits *Newsnight*. What does he actually think?

Prince Charles
When Mummy finally abdicates or pops her clogs it's going to be Charles III, so get ready. New coins, new stamps, new-age King.

David Beckham
David should concentrate all his attention on one thing: the 2006 World Cup. It's as simple as that Becks, son.

* The word 'Europeans' is used in a purely geographical sense. Any of the above-mentioned who happen to be British are in no way 'batting for the other side' to the best of our knowledge.